PRAISE FOR *NO CREDIT RIVER*

T0282181

"In *No Credit River*, Zoe Whittall pulls u[...] ment and alienation, eros and elegy, and [...] of love we can never fully inhabit or abandon. The softly abraded memories are mapped by an ars poetica that signals both an experimentation with form and a grief-tempered, arresting honesty. These poems are an exploration of connection and loss, and the bonds that fray and fortify the self. *No Credit River* is a testament to our queer and artistic communities—profoundly thoughtful, coursing with intelligence."
—ALI BLYTHE, author of *Stedfast*

"*No Credit River* is a masterful expression of queer heartache. Zoe Whittall writes with self-possessed and unmitigated emotion. She writes both with urgency and the sagacity that comes with a dark-night-of-the-soul level of reflection. The lyrical prose firmly holds the weight of the book's themes. I love the gutsy musicality of the writing. I am particularly moved by Whittall's use of motif and refrain to remind us of the cyclical nature of love and grief and healing."
—AMBER DAWN, author of *My Art Is Killing Me and Other Poems*

"Whittall's return to poetry has been well worth the wait. Call this a collection of prose poems, call it autofiction, call it memoir riddled with metaphor, call it names, call it whatever you want really, as long as you call it. These poems embrace contradiction like lovers who have broken up but still won't let go; they fill the wasteland between the phrases 'nothing is traumatic' and 'everything is traumatic.' *No Credit River* is one of the most electrifying collections I have read in years."
—HANNAH GREEN, author of *Xanax Cowboy*

no credit river

Zoe Whittall

Book*hug Press
Toronto 2024

FIRST EDITION

Library and Archives Canada Cataloguing in Publication

Title: No credit river / Zoe Whittall.
Names: Whittall, Zoe, author.
Identifiers: Canadiana (print) 2024034555X | Canadiana (ebook) 20240345568
  ISBN 9781771669078 (softcover)
  ISBN 9781771669160 (EPUB)
Subjects: LCGFT: Autobiographical poetry. | LCGFT: Prose poems. | LCGFT: Poetry.
Classification: LCC PS8595.H4975 N6 2024 | DDC C811/.6—dc23

The production of this book was made possible through the generous assistance of the Canada Council for the Arts and the Ontario Arts Council. Book*hug Press also acknowledges the support of the Government of Canada through the Canada Book Fund and the Government of Ontario through the Ontario Book Publishing Tax Credit and the Ontario Book Fund.

Book*hug Press acknowledges that the land on which we operate is the traditional territory of many nations, including the Mississaugas of the Credit, the Anishnabeg, the Chippewa, the Haudenosaunee, and the Wendat peoples. We recognize the enduring presence of many diverse First Nations, Inuit, and Métis peoples, and are grateful for the opportunity to meet and work on this territory.

"In general poems are pathetic and diaries are pathetic.
Really literature is pathetic.
Ask anyone who doesn't care about literature."
—Eileen Myles

"What doesn't kill you makes you weird at intimacy"
—Ely Kreimendahl

For Mudball

Contents

SECTION THREE

Ars Poetica / Poem in the Form of a Note Before Reading

IT IS A CONFUSING THING to be born between generations where the one above thinks nothing is trauma and the one below thinks everything is trauma. I don't like any new smell. An alarm out of nowhere. A gritty texture. I hate wind. I like the fifth-grade definition of best friend. I like certainty. The types of uncertainty I can abide by: not knowing which point of view to choose, slipping between narrating with authority and curiosity. I love to guess at second person, get a white dress dirty in the summer, not knowing as I fasten each clasp that morning if the day will be fun enough for a muddy hemline. I like the danger of eavesdropping, and spontaneous group singing, looking around and wondering who might dance with me. I like sustaining a bit, crass art, an anthemic bridge that bests the chorus, and I like to be in love.

Of course a poet likes to be in love. To fall for someone you have to be vulnerable, to hold a teaspoon of existential terror in your mouth and let it go. Intimacy is the only cliff jump I like. Otherwise I'm in a lifelong battle with catastrophic thinking. On his podcast the comedian Marc Maron says the only risks he takes are emotional and I pull over to write that down. Oversimplified attachment theory memes on the internet would say the anxiously attached person is just as afraid of intimacy as her avoidant partner but has someone else to blame for the distance. I started writing this book and stopped prioritizing love because I had a broken heart that bordered on lunacy. That's a poetic exaggeration but also not. In the spring of 2021 my therapist, through Zoom, said, You're doing well. You really seem like you have it together. I was telling her that it had been two years since the breakup and I still felt grief. I was holding stones in my palm, telling myself their heaviness was the relationship, and throwing them into the lake to let them go. I watched them sink like a wilful tangible metaphor but they didn't help. If my therapist is the person I tell the worst things to, and she says I'm doing well post-breakup and miscarriage and rewatching the same *Gilmore Girls* or *Grey's Anatomy* every night over and over, then how can you ever be perceived?

Who you are when you're alone is who you really are. I had five months between the most distressing breakup of my life and the onset of the pandemic. I can't believe my therapist doesn't know me after three years, I told the kitten who was born the month my baby would have been born in another, luckier timeline. Once, in San Francisco, in a relationship I had expanded past its true lifespan, I read the sentence *No adult can abandon another adult*, from the codependency reader in Michelle Tea's bathroom. I mention her full name because she's a brilliant, funny writer and her work often touches on the passion and traumas particular to queer relationships. I suppose this book is, in a way, one that touches on the passion and traumas of queer relationships. I felt abandoned, and I felt it for years. You can feel things that aren't true, and then it's extra embarrassing to admit those feelings when they come up. After two years I decided to move to a small town where for the better part of the year everyone around me is on vacation. I don't know where you are, and finally I don't want to. The important thing is I am here, and I can get up and be standing in a lake in about ten minutes any time I like, where none of the stones are you.

Nadine Gordimer said that writing is making sense of life. It is hard to find writing about femme and trans masc relationships, and in what does exist the femme point of view is often suspect, or the text is discussed as suspect. I'm not trying to argue about *The Argonauts* (though I love it) or relive the days of SOFFA support groups or Strap-On.org infighting (which passed the time in my night shift early twenties) or claim any kind of cis femme oppression nonsense (I'm over the way we treated butches, mascs, and trans men—though I'm not conflating those terms—as though they never experience/d misogyny), but I am thinking that there is nothing brave about *not* trying to write about it.

After all, I didn't begin my literary career writing papers about Robertson Davies; I wrote zines about sex and poems about Kathy Acker. Do you have the right to write about this, we asked ourselves while stapling perzines together or in MFA workshops. Trying to write honestly about the complications of living in a world that misunderstands both of you and actively hates the trans partner, considers both of your identities to be false or fake or monstrous, is difficult. There is an urge to protect your community from outsiders who think we're all crazy and are looking for evidence. But there's a reason I'm not a scholar, and it's mostly about language. I've been trying to write this paragraph all day and looked up Joan Nestle quotes about twelve times. And how do you write a love story without thinking of the audience? Who mostly won't get it, but is that a freedom?

No one at my funeral will say *She was always so much fun.* Is this book going to be me leaning into my Annie Ernaux era? Part of what drew me to him was that he was also anxious. But about different things.

This book covers a few years leading up to meeting in 2014, and the years after we parted in August 2019. That first January he sent me a photo of a heart drawn in the sand on a beach in Thailand and the words *I've decided we're having a love affair.* He read one of my novels on the plane there and another on the way back. I mean, if you want to woo a writer it's impossible to think of a better strategy. A few weeks later he sent me a text that read, *I am your boyfriend. It's all I want to be.* I didn't stop to think. I don't think I had a single thought for the next six months.

I read everything labelled autofiction but I hadn't ever written it. This is my first crack at it. A narrator with my name, moving slowly through a plotless day, thinking about ideas. But I'm neither a waif who attended an Ivy League school nor a rugged man, and beauty is so much a part of the form. I am not enigmatic or without social media and I don't know how to dress in a way that looks like I may spend half the year in Paris. I can't attempt to write slyly about power in heterosexual relationships because I was a queer in the nineties and we made art porn for fun and politics and something to do. But I'm drawn to autofiction in an attempt at an alienated truth. I am inspired by the New Narrative movement, Dodie Bellamy in particular, or the New York School poets with their wit and flowing stream of consciousness. I have curled-up, dog-eared copies of *Women* by Chloe Caldwell, *300 Arguments* by Sarah Manguso on my bedside table. This is an unreliable memoir, in prose poetry. And if you picture this book as a long string, I clipped off the most ecstatic memories on one end and the most horrid on the other. They're in a green notebook, in a box in the attic next to torn fabric and pink ribbons from the type of chocolates he used to buy me on Valentine's that he now buys for someone else.

Not writing about the worst things means I don't have to adhere to any expected act structure. Autofiction permits stories without villains. There is only a made-up recipe, mostly style and feelings. This is a book of ideas, I imagine saying, ideas about attachment or devotion or loss or being pathetic. Or a beautiful book of ugliness. Readers might say nothing happens as though it weren't by design.

He once told me that someone he broke up with stopped dating for a decade after he left her. I could not understand why—why stay single for that long? But now I understand it. I don't mean that he was a bad partner and I was a good partner. That is not how relationships work, or at least it is not an interesting way to write about relationships.

And maybe I should do like Marguerite Duras and wait until I'm seventy to write this. Or, maybe like Rachel Cusk, sit on an airplane and tell you the story of the guy sitting next to me and mention my divorce in a passing sentence. I didn't want to write about it, but how do you stop yourself? Artists get the hands they're dealt. You just have to play the hell out of them.

A Shot at the Night

I.

When we first started dating you said, *If you want me to smell like anything in particular just leave that product in your shower.* I laughed that after twenty years of dating women it was the most heterosexual moment of my life. I wrote it in my joke notebook. The best comedy is someone telling you secrets. Most poets think that's the worst kind of poetry.

You can't heal in isolation, so I'm on a journey with a mid-morning squirrel, eating his breakfast peanuts on the backyard moss, the three o'clock sand dunes, the single trees I love, and the group of trees I fear for their ability to obscure a murderer, a body, a bear. I walk down the path and when I get what feels like too far I push myself to go a bit further. I'm trying to learn that being in the forest by yourself isn't just for men and wolves.

It's no wonder that the almost marriage between Mr. I'm Sorry Your Feelings Are Hurt and Ms. I Want What You Want (but will resent you for not giving me what I never admitted to want) didn't work out.

I remember you bent over a book in a beam of sunlight, underlining passages, your arm outstretched through the driver's side window to feed deer in Thunder Bay while telling childhood stories, the delight in your eyes while preparing carrot pie from *The Moosewood Cookbook*, your grin as you and the kids carry in a tray of birthday breakfast in bed. I never stopped feeling lucky. But maybe that was part of the problem. Is it luck that someone might want to love me?

In one of our last exchanges we accused each other of not knowing ourselves. We both said, *My astrologer said you were incapable of true introspection, of really knowing yourself.* It was the queerest moment of our relationship, to both start sentences with "My astrologer said."

No one writes poetry about somebody they don't miss.

But if writing is a way of letting someone go, putting it all into a book is a way of making sure they won't come back.

2.

I thought we had a great love. I thought I would never fail you. But that thought was my first failure, to not realize I was more than one thing, and you were more than one thing, that relationships involve failing and repairing, over and over, until you've built something strong together with the ropes of those frayed defeats. I did all the things I judge other people for, including writing about it.

Coco Ridge

THIS IS A POEM FROM before we met. I barely remember that person. It was back when people weren't especially interested in pliable memory. You shouldn't tell readers what you can show. A group of us went away to a thinning cabin. Swimsuit straps thick against femme shoulders, wet shirts on the butches darkened blue like this Kawartha lake. The city remained a burr adhered to an acrylic blanket. Some of us got dock-rock, a swirling feeling. Paperback spines split open, fading in the sun: *Whipping Girl, A Visit from the Goon Squad, White Teeth*. Our thirties were a rush in and out. Without the internet, it's a Grade 7 dance. Everyone does salvia. Except me, of course. I am always uncomfortable in the world but I rarely do drugs that threaten my baseline disquiet. Instead I make summer salads and hug the wall. Fresh mint sliced with a haggard knife. Basil ripped on tomato tops. The awkward sway of a handmade dress. I worried the other couples could hear us fight behind a thin clapboard wall. I didn't know she was a fighter when we first got together, though she was country and country girls fight. On our first date she drove us home drunk, one of those Gen X moral quandaries, with enough vodka that we remember being seventeen in a truck on a dirt-road roller coaster. The euphoria that is ideation in the moderate morning. I look at everyone hallucinating on the orange shag carpet and know that many of us will not divorce easily and the future is a tornado outstretched into wilful submission. When we know we should break up we get matching tattooed flowers instead.

A few months later I am in the grocery store when I end up behind you in line. I am getting divorced, I say. Me too, you respond. We

9

were not actually married but we had rings. One she lost in another woman's car. I used to work the door at a bar, and when you would walk in, my whole body would seize up. That was when I was twenty-five. Before I'd even spoken a word to you. After I unpack my groceries I send a note: *would you like to have a drink?* It is the kind of bravery born of nothing left to lose. When you say *yes* I dance around my kitchen and make a list on the back of a bank slip of every calorie I consumed that day.

One couple from the cottage trip is still together, but they've got a girlfriend in Hungary and they sleep with Skype open so it's as though she's beside them. She's very demanding and no one in Canada likes her but maybe a throuple is better than divorce. A poem is four hundred years of lesbian gossip.

You Get on Planes Anyway, Despite the Fear

YOU HAVE A BOOK OF translations in Brussels. You have climbed up onto the roof to take photos in Brussels. You have twelve days left of touring in Brussels. You realize your parents never taught you how to travel in Brussels. You have an itchy throat and variant paranoia in Brussels. You are in room 426 at the Hotel Atlas in Brussels. You read about YouTube composer Nico Muhly in Brussels. You reproduce only what you understand in Brussels. You are annoyed that writers are considered public intellectuals in Brussels. You go to lunch with a painter and a diplomat in Brussels. You don't know which fork to use in Brussels. You have a girlfriend you don't feel like fighting with in Brussels. You anaesthetize your tonsils with black cherry lozenges in Brussels. You do not correspond with Elizabeth Bishop in Brussels. You have twelve days left of touring in Brussels. You do not know how Asia feels about the book in Brussels. You cannot speak without a slow fade in Brussels. You have stopped short of crying out twice in Brussels.

You are in room 426 at the Hotel Atlas in Brussels. You wonder about kissing a man with a bruised shoulder in Brussels. You say *oiseau* with a shy Montreal accent in Brussels. You flirt with the other poet on tour in Brussels. You cannot translate the problems with monogamy in Brussels. You have twelve days left of touring in Brussels. You are happy to comment on that in Brussels. You autograph your name on the title page with a spelling error in Brussels.

Do We Know a Jeremy?

WHAT IS VIRTUE ANYWAY? AFTER a night shift as a paramedic my girlfriend swallows a melatonin pill and climbs into bed; the sun rises as we pull the heavy curtains together. I creep through a morning routine. On the kitchen counter a handwritten note reads, *I saved a man from overdosing on heroin tonight I think we know him from somewhere. Do we know a Jeremy?* I turn the note over and write, *To-Do.* Today my tasks are simple. Boil the chicken carcass for soup and write a short story. Make some short grain rice and broccolini to pack in Tupperware for her second night shift; remember to be lucid, notice the details, describe the room, respect the reader, cut the carrots so she won't choke, soften the onions, dollop the yogourt.

I clutch a rounded mug of coffee while she sleeps, on either side of fate and wish. All failed concepts. What is virtue anyway? On Saturday I sat at home watching reality TV while she did CPR on the side of the highway. I joke about how there's no greater illustration of the disparity between our societal worth. When she wakes up at 4 p.m. she tells me that after she saved the guy she put the heroin in her pocket. But didn't it almost kill him? I'm stockpiling, she says, for when we're really old. It will be a great way to go out. You're going to be the most popular old lady in the retirement home, I say, as though she doesn't know that.

The Curse of Dupont Subway Station

I WAKE UP LIKE I always do, wondering if I should have a baby. This week a train derailed, killing three and injuring sixty. A ticket collector at our subway station was shot in the neck. I wake up tense, like I always do, wondering if I'm in the wrong movie. I am not naturally a tense person. I wonder if my asthma medication makes me this way; if it's my girlfriend, do I absorb her stress? Flawed and tired of my mid-thirties, I don't want my friends to die. This is the decade when it begins: slowly people fall away, one after the other in a senseless tumble. Biking in the sun without sleeves is a miracle, a salve. I like knowing my friend Lisa has had the same phone number for ten years. It's the only one I have memorized besides my childhood party line. Today our heads pirouetted for a madman in Norway; Amy Winehouse dead at twenty-seven from booze.

I have four slices of apple, a boiled egg, red jam in a small white saucer, a circle of pepper and salt drawn on the plate. I'm trying to write a novel and a film. The table next to me is pregnant, the table to my left breastfeeding; nobody reads anymore.

Neurotic, Bisexual, Alberta

THERE IS AN ELK OUTSIDE my room at the Banff Centre. I write for her, a series of chapters where I make my characters active. They open doors and ride bikes and have sex and make Popsicles in plastic moulds for make-believe children. They get so active I forget about the language. Form is content, I tell the elk. My girlfriend and I have an arrangement, a type of freedom whenever we travel. This makes me consider all strangers from a different angle. When I'm the one left at home it makes me sleepless and on edge. I go to see Dave read from a new play. I watch Jonathan give a talk. When I'm with a woman, I look only at men, and vice versa. You should know you're bisexual if you answer the question *Are you ever just happy with what you've got?* I know gender isn't that simple. But maybe this passing interest in cis men is just about the kid thing, about the countdown to thirty-five. It can't be about masculinity because my girlfriend could kill Jonathan in a fist fight. I think about how everyone says that no one ever thinks they're ready to have a kid. The only artist here with a child looks frighteningly alive to be alone with her manuscript. Jonathan and I talk about our relationship problems, and about the famous Canadian poet who has propositioned us both for threesomes. When I walk into town, down the little forest path, in my green spring dress and dry skin, everyone I encounter has a bear bell. They ring with every step like human churches on a Sunday morning. Trees, rocks, animals—they're all larger in the West. Louder. More dangerous. The beauty here has a scale too immense to take in with one glance. I don't wear a bell. I didn't think of it. This makes me happy. I am always thinking about the risk of death. When a slip of me could be slightly easygoing, I brag to myself about myself. I see the elk again and say, Look at me, taking chances. Tell the bear to come at me.

I Don't Know Where I'm Flying Until I Get to the Airport

I HAND THE AGENT MY ticket, expecting to go to Regina but it's for Saskatoon. It's the most Toronto moment of my life and I'm ashamed with my red purse full of ChapStick and downers and breath mints. In Moose Jaw I have a spider bite on my arm that grows, glowing pink into red, and the pharmacist says it's nothing to worry about but I do. I give readings and think about my arm the whole time. The redness gets hot to the touch and reaches my elbow, which the internet says isn't good. I'm worried it's going to start speaking to me. I always choose to worry, especially about dying of sepsis in a Moose Jaw hotel room before I've had a chance to have a baby. That's not my third act! A reporter asks me to hold my book so that he can take a photo, and the next day it's on the front page of the newspaper. There is a hot pool on the roof of the hotel. I talk to a writer about her toddler at home. I talk to another single woman about how she wants to have a kid soon too. I look around at the afterparty and I think, Perhaps this is my chance. I'm only allowed to look for a fling but I'm subconsciously looking for a co-parent. But my worry beams from me. No one is attracted to the anxious. And mostly writers aren't attractive to other writers, it's like two tops or two solipsists. When I meet straight married writers I can always tell which one has had their dreams crushed while doing the dishes for a partner with a literary prize on a shelf in a basement office. I go back to my room to read. If I always choose to read, my memoir will be mundane, I realize, running a finger down the room service menu after cracking another spine.

Ten years later, before editing this old poem, I am sitting in the green chair by the window on Yarmouth Road during the second lockdown. I find out the woman with the toddler, now a tween, has a dire cancer diagnosis. The other woman is out on bail for trying to protect her child from an abusive father. I bring home a kitten born the month I was supposed to give birth. At the Moose Jaw airport all the writers pull out their notebooks when the flight is delayed and say, *I can't wait to read your new book,* to each other like the *peace be with you* mumble in church.

Tell Me How You Know What You Know

YOU DIDN'T REALIZE THE APOLOGY plant was plastic; I watered it for two weeks before I noticed. On Halloween you said, Let's watch scary movies about snakes, or zombies, or intimacy. Eight years old, playing hide-and-seek: while your friend counted to ten, you just walked home. West of Winnipeg, the rain was within sight, so you drove for forty-five minutes to catch it. South of Big Sur, we are thirty-nine in a rented guest suite with a pool. You are almost a doctor. We are a swarm of secrets in good salt. Your two fears: being smothered, being abandoned. San Luis Obispo, an infinity pool: you're the teacher, the no-boundaries boss, the skater with two criminals for friends. My fears: open spaces, literal powerlessness.

Your sons don't like surprises. The river rises, the youngest grabs my hand. I'm the shoreline's soft shoulder, tolerating uncertainty. We are suddenly the adults now? I tattoo his tiny arm with a pink pony, feel my hips and mouth sharpen, ready to fight off any danger.

Thirty-nine, without a baby, a female body becomes indecipherable, to the waitress at Montana's, our extended family, and now even the other queers. When we walk the tender red landscape in Arizona, I stand at the altar for dead husbands and children at the base of the mountain. I count to ten. I think you are hiding, but you rise behind the saguaro, alone.

Sunset Junction Pantoum

FALLING ASLEEP IN YOUR SOFTENING chokehold in a Silverlake guest house. When you visit, we flit between detachment and the best sex of our lives. While hiking in Topanga, I can never move or breathe right. I cringe at how you had to pretend I wasn't always disappointing you.

When you visit, we flit between detachment and the best sex of our lives. I can hide my dead tooth when I smile. I cringe at how you had to pretend I wasn't always disappointing you. In the mornings I get into a stranger's Lexus that idles on Hyperion.

I can hide my dead tooth when I smile. We winnow through the dry stone gullies of Hollywood. In the mornings I get into a stranger's Lexus that idles on Hyperion. Eyes in the rear-view: Is your husband here too? Why are you alone?

We winnow through the dry stone gullies of Hollywood. I whisper Normandie, Vermont, Heliotrope, Sunset, or the 101? Eyes in the rear-view: Is your husband here too? Why are you alone? No one warns you how cold it is in LA, I reply, willing a new conversation.

I whisper Normandie, Vermont, Heliotrope, Sunset, or the 101? This block is dangerous, you shouldn't be alone here. No one warns you how cold it is in LA, I reply, willing a new conversation. Falling asleep in your softening chokehold in a Silverlake guest house.

I'd Like a Double Espresso and The National on Repeat

THE FIRST TIME YOU BROKE up with me I sat in the window at the Hub café on Dovercourt watching couples walk their dogs, push strollers, hold each other's drinks while they tied new spring sneakers. I was trying to work on my novel but was incapable of complex thought. Instead I took notes of things in front of me: a glass cup of purple clovers, *The Argonauts* in hardback that I carried with me everywhere in the summer of 2015, two silver pens from the country inn I thought of as our place. I held on to the coffee spoon, the mug, in case I flew away. I was aware of how close the café was to your ex-wife's house but I'd been coming to this café often, for years before I'd even met you, and had never seen her. Alison asked me, How are you? We had our laptops open to page one. I cried in response, involuntary. This is the state I was in when your ex approached my table. I was so shocked to see her as she said, If you ever want to talk about him, let me know. The way she said it was like she was trying to tell me you were complicated, and that maybe she could help me understand why. I loved the way you were complicated. I couldn't think of you as having any flaws at all. Is it not a flaw that he breaks up with you all the time, a friend asks.

It is impossible to recall how stupid you become when you're in love, after it is over. The memories are so illogical, like recalling how you stood still waiting for a car to hit you, like *No, it's fine, the car is fine.*

You read passages from *The Call of Character* to me. We had such similar outlooks, both emerging from difficult relationships we'd assumed would carry into our old age despite major incompatibilities. That summer we were apart, we still kept sleeping together. I felt ashamed to admit it to anyone. We got back together at Karine's wedding after I gulped white wine and failed at small talk because I couldn't stop my eyes from following you around the room.

Now Alison's book was published two years ago, and I can't even remember which novel I was working on that day, and the author of *The Call of Character* has just passed away too young, and I slide the book off my shelf, the yellow cloth hardback I stole from you. And I read the passages you underlined and mourn the memory of sitting on my old couch, listening to you talk about the value of breaking through the cultural fog that insists on relentless positivity.

Between the Love Bomb and the Free Fall

IN 2015, YOU SHOW UP at my door in a suit on your way to give a talk to tell me this time you are sure that it is over. The novel that will change my whole future is spread out in manuscript pages on the floor of the apartment. I spend the summer trying to date other people, find someone who might want to have a family. I try not to text you, but you call from your cabin where you've gone to be alone and we keep sleeping together in a way that makes me embarrassed to admit to my friends. Me for connection, and you for a reason I can't explain but feels like heartlessness even though I know that isn't true. In September we get back together at a friend's wedding, right before I leave for Los Angeles. You take me canoeing north of the city. My new goal is to stop thinking catastrophically. If I stop to take a breath I think, *I'm finally where I want to be.* My book sells, and we are growing closer, not just in a honeymoon blur but in ways that feel anchoring. On the plane ride home from Los Angeles I feel as though I'm flying back to you, to be part of your family. Your youngest son falls asleep in the car and I stare at the headlights on the 401 as they blur and I want to cozy into winter with all of you. This time I know for sure, you say. You ask me, in a hot spring north of the city on my fortieth birthday, if I'd join your family.

The day before, I had thought you were going to leave. My friends stepped in and planned a party for me because they thought you weren't going to do anything, assuming you were going to break up with me again. All day I felt grateful for my friends, and I tried to be happy about at least having them, even if I was never going to have you and this life I'd imagined, sitting in my apartment waiting for you to show up for dinner an hour late.

How to Fail as a Comedy Writer and a Wife

MOVING TO LOS ANGELES AND failing is the most Canadian thing I've ever done. I wasn't being funny, which was my job, nor was I tolerating loneliness or successful at becoming friends with competitive comedy writers. I loved the flowers but not the rats that hang out in the blossoming trees. The posters on the corner of Hyperion and Sunset are trying to convince me to try a tapeworm for weight loss. TV writing has its own jargon. A hat on a hat. Let's blue-sky this. I used the word *competitive* above but I meant *cruel*. All the fresh juice is filled with charcoal. I spend my first weekend going nowhere except Trader Joe's. I accidentally wander into *Scandal* filming B-roll on my way to eat secret lunch on the lot. My ego isn't big enough to be here, I tell my best friends at home who work in offices, but my body is too big. I'd been working alone in a room writing a novel for so many months that I forgot how mean a boss could be. I rented an actor's garage. Feral cats lived on the roof. I tried to feed them every morning but we never bonded. I'm just trying to be myself in a city of people trying to be other people, I tell the bravest feral, as he puts one paw into a yogourt container filled with 5 a.m. tap water.

Vestibular Autumn

I SHOULD GO STAND IN the sun. This is the final day. No doubt it is almost winter, almost hanging time. I want a weighted blanket, a warm cup with a thumb mould. I woke up with vertigo. The world is the same but the ground is softer, the air porous. A still body, but a mind doing a somersault down the hall.

The doctor says, Don't look up or down. Which is easier than it sounds. I should go stand in the sun. Will it rinse the dizziness from my face? At dinner the eleven-year-old teaches the six-year-old about angles. Do you know what an angle is? The six-year-old lies and says yes. All I see in their tender faces are the angles, the glare off the yellow kitchen walls.

I lean into my partner's plaid shirt. I want to see his face but I can't look up. This vertigo is about my inner ear, but it feels like my regular head problems. I have meetings that could Make My Career but I am half-present,, counting four, five, six to make sure I get enough oxygen on the inhale. I should cross the street, stand in the sun. But I don't want to spin and drop into traffic.

I meet an old friend I used to struggle with. We get our nails done. We used to be broke and aspiring. Now we have money, enough to pay fifty dollars for a manicure that won't chip for weeks. We made every penny from writing down things we think about other things. The veracity of each nail, the thick unyielding matte, is hopeful. It's the part of me that's solid.

I admire it, this pretending at the tip of each finger. How long can I go on having this long nervous breakdown of a life? I was born in a snowstorm, the hospital two hours away. The closest farm was a speck on the horizon. Now I find the dog park across the street too vast. The city makes you think that having other people around means you're safe. When you grow up in the country, the adults tell you that safety is about being one of a select few. I stumble up the stairs. *Do you worry about looking drunk?* the questionnaire asks. I circle Y but would it make me look younger? I'm too anxious to get drunk.

I should stand in the sun.

It's just over there.

Stolen Daylight

I DID NOT WRITE ANYTHING today except my name on a contract that I did not read. It is thick November. The rain is pushy, over-the-top. I am eating a half-hearted kiwi. One uneven slice slicks the floor, more dirty yellow than green, more grit than sweet. Nothing is the right rhythm now. There is a lockdown at a school nearby. Too near the kids that aren't mine but whose cereal bowls I wash three days a week. In the fall, I fall apart and you find May unbearable. Is he emotionally neglectful or are you just an awful person? Are you unbearable to be around? Are you not trying hard enough to meet his needs? Are your needs too great? When I leave the house and people are nice to me, interested in me, I accidentally drive my bike into traffic.

At the End of Summer, You Suggest We Get Married

I HAVE NEVER WANTED A wedding, though I have often thought marriage would be a comfortable container. At the end of summer we were driving between small-town literary festivals, and you said that you would like to marry me. I tried to make my face neutral. I smiled to the window streaked from sticky children's hands. We decided to ask Zohar to be the one to marry us, discussed how small we could make the party and still meet the definition of a wedding. We go to a beach and I'm wearing a white bikini top and bright pink lipstick, and I only remember those specifics because I stared so often at the photos I took that day, remembering the hot sand, the cloudless sky, the pop of hopeful feeling.

When we get home you trap a giant cockroach under a coconut yogourt container, and it's still there three days later. The cats circle it. We move around it, getting coffee, eating cereal, before we write toward page counts in our rooms. When you plan to get married, maybe it's good to know who is the one who can kill; who can follow through on the undesirable tasks of living. It turns out we both half-way handle things and then get stuck examining the metaphorical, wishing it away. Is the bug dead yet? Not yet. What does it mean? We don't lift the container.

Two years later, a month before you left me, you spilled yogourt over the gearshift of your car and never cleaned it. You must have thought every day, *I should take care of that*, and then closed the door and forgot. By the time I drive boxes of fragile things to my new apartment, it's just a gritty white stain, a part of the car.

We both got official ADHD diagnoses after we broke up. I wonder if this will allow us some perspective, grace, or ease if we ever try to talk it through.

But we won't.

Big Deal Literary Awards

IS MY FACE MAKING THE right expression? I whisper, as the cameras pan to us, the scholar and the novelist. We sit beside a wealthy heiress. She is filthy with jewels, a smeared lip, the open-hearted glow of an eccentric. She says to you, I have never met a transsexual, this is delightful! All around us artists and millionaires intersect. I see a once-disgraced politician who dragged a bike courier to death with his BMW. I see the MVP authors who have learned to walk this runway with ease. In all of the photos our faces are purple and shiny, under heat lamps, warming like baby chicks.

We wake up the morning after at the Ritz-Carlton hotel. A TV inside the bathroom mirror plays a Whit Stillman movie. I punch my gown and lapel flower into a No Frills bag before I wrestle my bike from a thief, cycle home through the crunch of dying leaves. I pause at the dog park to flirt with a Boston terrier, a hapless spaniel. I find my consolation prize money in a hunk of one hundred clustered bobby pins. I spend the money fixing a dead tooth.

Later I will watch a recording of the ceremony, but I'll only be able to zero in on my arms, larger than arms are generally permitted to be on TV. I'll recall the pitying look in the skinny author's eyes, whose book had the word *fat* in the title, after an audience member assumed her novel was mine. I thought about writing, *Being fat is kind of great sometimes, it's like an invisibility superpower, but I didn't write this book. This character hates herself, but I don't.*

Not exactly true, but it's a persuasive thing to say, that will eventually become true if you repeat it enough. If you refuse the humiliation foisted upon your body every time you leave the house, eventually it's just a warm rain, a lifting fog, a background hiss. One that you know is slowly killing you, but what else can you do but blend and float and wake up every morning entwined with someone who understands you, who in the best moments of your relationship makes you feel like you've won the lottery with your body's best flaws? And, in the worst moments, can wield that vulnerable knowledge like a weapon? We both make this mistake.

After the gala, where we didn't know how to stand or how to sit, we snuck up to the hotel pool, closed our eyes and jumped, revelled in the bliss and humility of feeling so lucky, our formal wear soaked, a dream floating away.

April Tornado Watch

COFFEE LID THE COLOUR OF a pinched lip, a spring so avoidant I'm attracted to it. This rain is wet-whispering a menacing taunt. Because a tornado took our barn in 1983, I am untethered by wind. I don't like the wind, I say, as I make origami hearts on the living room carpet. We got the rug thick, so we could sink into the floor, so it would call us to nap. I order blush and Victorian nightgowns that come in the mail. I pick up my phone between lines. I scroll to feel the weight of me lift. I know he's beside me but he isn't. He's with all the followers. I can never be as simultaneously far away and close as they are. I am just here, in parallel play, with our phones out and our bodies on pause, the wind throwing elbows outside.

Millcroft Marriage

DURING A FULL MOON, OYSTERS close and dogs bite. We stand on wet cedar by the river, watching geese dunk their feathery, restless heads. I'm longing for you and you are longing to be by yourself. I don't realize, thick in spring mud, that this is our last visit. In the afternoon we crest the deep end of the pool, splay on single beds of bleached towels. Books fanned out, spines split. There's a fake peacock in the ficus, a soft whir of the hot-tub filter. From here I can see the first room we ever checked into, back when we couldn't keep our clothes on. Deer nosed the window of the second room. You had a checkered tie. A few years later we brought your mothers to the dining room window that overlooked the falls. We rode oddly shaped rental bikes into the village. There are photos of you on the hill, face obscured by the softness of dusk, looking down at me. I remember giving my credit card to the front desk and not caring what they charged. On my fortieth birthday in the salt pool, you invited me to join your family. The water nearing immolation temperature, but it was the best moment of my life, so I didn't move, stayed and got dizzy, my body telling me it wasn't right, but had I ever listened to the thing I drag my brain around in? The next year I sat in a third-floor windowsill when a movie producer called. We had a room in the guest house to celebrate your PhD. I made you a shirt with the word *Doctor* on it. On this final visit, was it just the mundanity of domesticity? I kept the free roses they'd throw on the bed, those crisp red fists in the bottom of a discarded silver purse. Before checkout, we wander the hallways of the hotel like we're saying hi to the ghosts of some great love, but not ours.

Insistence on Sameness

OH I HAVE BEEN HERE before. It's a comfort, when I remember a
hotel lobby, a main street, the way the wind can be summer warm
for a winter hour in Calgary. I buy cowboy boots and order a steak
with Alison in the hotel restaurant. I press heavy tines into mashed
potatoes while we gossip about writers we know, confess our hopes
and failures. Her debut novel had a line about canoeing that I still
think about fifteen years later.

I have been here before. The arrivals gate. This stretch of the 401
home, backpack full of signed copies. And back on the red couch,
I have met him before, this man who sits beside me, like a stranger
on a bench. We own this couch together, and we've made a life, and
now he's not sure. Maybe this isn't what works for him. He comes
and goes as he pleases, and I wait. Warm all the time, just waiting.

No Credit River

LACES THREAD THROUGH RUSTED-OUT EYELETS, boot scuffed from chain-guard kicks. You show up in a suit, offer a relentless pound of condescending words uttered in monotone.

The lake flickers noon waves this way, that way, out a ways. It's a floor, a false bottom, the oblivion of thin water. He is living on a river now miles away, no running water: a modern hermit, a scholar of solitude.

I visited twice, heels scuffed on the attic ceiling. Palms down in the dirty river, forcing apart the brambles to lay over the small stones that could slight us, he looked upstream while I gripped the wild grasses, river-washed pebbles on my tongue.

This is the kind of manicure that doesn't come off. The day I noted its sheen gripping someone else's shoulder was the day I knew he wasn't gone from me, *the best way to get over is to get under* is a lie. I shut the door and cried.

He showed up the next day. I looked at my fingers against his plaid shirt. How much better each nail looked against his ideal body, how much better he looked than anyone else, the soft love in his voice.

He must have sensed the other person somehow. He was always so territorial in a way that made me light-headed, pliable, durable whenever he said, You're mine, forcing legs apart, bramble cuts, soft currents, the glory of belonging to him.

Just one more time. Could we make it count? This river eroding, this simple ending, this choking sound, the fox that darts behind the cabin, his hand on my skirt in the Brampton supermarket, I couldn't wait, we couldn't stop the monstrous feeling, this abject desire, from doing me in.

There'll Be No Knock on the Door

ALEX WOULD HAVE LOVED THIS mint-and-cauliflower taco. She would have loved this owl cup, this espresso. We are in a small city, we park everywhere for free, we can lock up, lucky, and just go. I biked by the old apartment and remembered how much my cat hated her cat, and how much her cat didn't care. I remember we jogged around Christie Pits when we had sad days.

I wanted to call her the night of the final Hip show. She was still alive then, I can't believe I didn't call. I sat between my aging parents, who didn't know the band, and a five-year-old who was bored. I was without courage. I was trying to get through the stress of living this amazing life full of love, I remember crying during "Grace, Too" when Gord cried, seeing the fear of death in his face. I find out about her death on my way to be on national radio. I cry up until the *and we're live* light goes on. Then I get on a plane to Winnipeg, where you are waiting in arrivals with a special candle to burn, and I watch its flame on top of the room service menu binder in our hotel room. We walk by the river with your old friend who is having delusions. I watch how well you care for them. I am struck with this feeling of luck to be loved so well by you, and to watch you care for others.

A few months later I see her mom. She said that when Leonard Cohen died, Alex said, *I hope we're on the same train*. Right before she died, she said, *I want some water*. And they gave her a glass. And she said, *No, I want the good stuff*, so they gave her bottled water. And she said, *No, the good stuff*. And they said, *What do you mean?* and she said, *I want peace*.

Sea Heart

THERE'S THE WAY I LIVE, and the way I think I live. I sat on our porch reading an Irish novel about an affair. The protagonist was twenty-one but wiser than I'll ever be. You were inside finishing the dishes after I'd steamed carrots and baked fish. When I was clearing some plates, I thought about the novel. The passages about longing made me feel as though I were living in greyscale. On the TV show the therapist says, Was it because of his impenetrable indifference? The women cry a lot on this show, they are all unhappy. The men are handsome and distant. The women are sad and mean. We ask his son if he'd like to speak at his school pride circle. He says, But our family isn't LGBT. I explain, Yes, your father is trans and I am queer. But I don't admit that we pass as cis and straight. The world treats us that way and, even at eight years old, he knows that. We get in the car and I can't stop myself from crying at the pride circle. Imagine hearing this at eight? What would it be like, if we'd known we were fine? If being queer and trans in the 1980s had been celebrated, would we fail less now? Odd to think of us as failing at anything, the year he wins the biggest scholarly award in the country, and I'm up for the biggest award in Canadian literature. I feel like I fell in here, to this straight life, after twenty years of being a dyke. But that's not true. I wanted it, even more than any award, any six-figure deal. After school his son and I draw chalk hearts on the sidewalk. There's the way I live and the way I want to live. He asked me to marry him and then stopped talking about it. There's the way I live and the way I want to live. I waited two years for him to bring it up again and he never did. I used to think this was all his fault, but I could have listened to the advice in that Kenny Rogers classic I used to sing it when I was eight, wandering around in the hayfields, trying not to fall into gopher holes.

Prince Edward County

AT THE ARTIST RETREAT I sleep under sloped farmhouse ceilings shaped like a tent, the slow draft in from a window overlooking cows lolling in a loose huddle. The kind of house that flexes metallic muscles in the night. The retreat dog is old and doesn't like me and I've tried everything to make him see my value. I think about how dogs can often sense illness or when someone is bad news. I'm not bad news, I whisper. I try to write my book but my eyes follow the tractor outside, up and down the field. I could be writing in a similar attic office in the city but you can't stand me anymore or it's just that you have to be alone to finish your PhD or you like me in small doses but accidentally invited me to live in your house. When I book the trips away by myself it's like I'm trying to hand you a present, and when you open it I fly up and away. I feel a hum of low resentment in our house. I can't tell if it's real or imagined, like the mould patterns on the attic wall; is this just what an old house is supposed to look and smell like? If our house in the city was rural it would be worth twenty dollars and because it's across from Trinity-Bellwoods it is probably 1.6 million like the house next door. The house next door is abandoned mid-renovation. I started putting peanuts on the bedroom window for the squirrels who live in it. You seem to only want me there when the children are home. I wash the dishes slower. I retreat upstairs. Now I'm in the country. While sitting at a beautiful wooden desk, I write about my grandmother in a rowboat in Turkey in 1922 as Smyrna burns. In real life I never had an honest or comfortable conversation with my grandmother, even though I lived with her for five years. I am there a week. I eat from plates of small sliced cucumbers, apples, cheese, and grapes. I am never at peace. This novel will never be what I wish it could be.

Four years later and single I move to the county, and I open the box of author copies of the book I was editing in that farmhouse retreat. I take photos of my face next to the brilliant colours on the cover. But the book isn't finished really, none of them are.

Sechelt

THERE IS A BEAR BETWEEN the theatre and the house a literary festival has rented for me. An orange cat outside, I seem to attract them everywhere I go. I try to get closer to him each day. I stand in the doorway, motioning him in while trying not to spill my coffee, away from the bear I know is roaming around. He refuses. By the end of the week I am able to give him a head scratch. A bear! I exclaim to the writers in the green room, but everyone is from the West Coast—seeing a bear is like seeing a coyote out east. You don't want to see them, but there is a sense of wonder when you do. I skim over a printout of my reading but can't help overhearing, He didn't do anything wrong. She was a student but she was as old as he was. I search for my lip balm and say, But it's a bear. A bear could eat you though? I pretend we're still having the conversation from earlier. I suppose so. I suppose it could.

Haliburton

WE RENT A COTTAGE FROM our famous friend. In the middle of the night, you accidentally fall down a flight of stairs because the door to the bathroom and the door to the stairs are side by side and easy to mistake. You are holding a glass of water, and the glass cuts you on your way down. We staunch the bleeding, and you almost pass out as I yell, Lie on the ground! Put your feet up! You look so fragile I am consumed by a terror I've never felt before. I never want to lose you, but I especially don't want to lose you from this earth because of the famous person's staircase. You say you are grateful I could take care of you. That I did well. This feedback fuels me for months. Years later when I miscarry, you call and say you wish you could help me the way I helped you. I wonder if you only say this because there is a pandemic and you can't come over to my house. That you are thinking this makes me fall in love again. It's a really stupid existence. I google how to stop being addicted to a person. I go outside and pick five wildflowers and put them under my pillow because a woman on Instagram says it will make me dream about the person I'm going to marry. I have another nightmare about you. I wake to see the cat with a skeletal daisy in his mouth.

Everyone Is a Tracy to Someone

I'VE ALWAYS HATED TRACY. IT'S been so long I can't remember why. I think she was cruel to a friend, and I've always held it against her. We were never friends. It's energetic, whatever the thing is. I can feel it in my spine whenever she's in my periphery. There's another Tracy I was neutral about until we became Facebook friends, and then I hated her. I hated every comment she ever made on a post. It burned in me, the feeling of seeing her name. Again, for no reason. Chemistry. I saw her on the street and she looked like a grandmother, and she's only a decade my senior. So I hated her for that, for reminding me of my age, of how we get slowly worse every year, less sharp, more Tracy. Though being older means I accept I am a Tracy to other people. I'm sure the sight of my trailing hemline, the crumbs on my breasts, the way I stand and text at the bus stop, somewhere someone is hating me.

Securely Attached

IF YOU LEAVE A SLICE of pineapple on your tongue, it will eventually make you bleed: the fruit you have to eat before it eats you. I get a message from a young author who tells me I write about breakups and heartbreak better than anyone else, that it's my "thing." I'm glad she made the comment online so she wouldn't see my irritated expression. When I answer her, I am sitting on the blue carpet you and I bought together for our home, extracting a sharp Lego piece from the bottom of my foot. I just published a family novel, a social novel, a book inspired by *The Corrections* in terms of the form— these are the phrases I repeat to journalists. (*The Corrections*, like *The Argonauts*, is a book no one is ambivalent about.) A domestic novel, I said to my agent over patio salads on the day we declare it officially complete. I send the younger writer a smiling emoji back and a thanks, though I want to say it's an old poem and I'm basically married now, my heartbreak verses in the past. Plus, my writing is all about anxiety. It's what poet Tony Hoagland would consider my irresolvable obsession, the one that all writers have. Like Emily Dickinson and her mortality, like Ryan Murphy's dancing teenagers trying to find unconditional love, like Susan Sontag and her closet-strangled pride.

Remember Me as a Revolutionary Communist

I WAS OBSESSED WITH US writing a book together, making a film, editing an anthology, creating some type of object that could be held. I want to say here, this is how it feels to have someone so close who could move me the way that you did. I felt too much happiness whenever we connected in conversation, or even just silently on the 407 to Brampton listening to Gillian Welch. If we had been musicians I'd have demanded duets, lines of improvised harmony, melody from the buzz between us when you would fall asleep and I would just watch your gorgeous face and think I had never felt happier to be anywhere. That my head against your chest was the best place I'd ever visited. I wanted to find all sorts of ways to have something that we made together because we would never have our own children. Everything at that time for me, as the days clipped toward forty, was about finding meaning in the absence of pregnancy. Which felt like a feminist failure, but perhaps that's not it at all. At times it was easy because I found so much meaning in you. That first year we did collaborate on a piece of art, a collage in tribute to Leslie Feinberg, for a charity art auction. I'd been asked to contribute something and I knew we could do something together. We used your photograph, silver duct tape, thick black marker, and the text of Feinberg's final words before they died, repeating. I don't know who bought it, but it comes up if you google both our names. It is fitting that neither of us owns it.

Baby Workshop

IN 2011 MY GIRLFRIEND AND 1 attend a Queers Planning Babies workshop. 1 plan to go by myself because I'm the only one who wants a kid. At the last minute she signs up as well. Our dilemma makes the workshop somewhat excruciating. The facilitators bring in a couple with a newborn baby. The dad in the couple is a guy I've had a crush on since 1 worked at the gay theatre and he used to come in occasionally. I'd told the bartender about my crush. You'd get along, he'd said. He's really sardonic, like you. I watch him hold the newborn. 1 am so jealous of the femme mom and so sad about my girlfriend and me—that she wants to do drugs and dance all night and I'm collecting cute baby shoes in a box under the bed. On the bike ride home, my girlfriend teases me about my crush on the dad. You blush around him, 1 can tell! 1 say nothing so that 1 don't lie. 1 feel bad, even though my girlfriend always has about three crushes at any given time. There is no way of knowing that when the baby is about to turn three, the couple will break up and I'll ask him out in a moment of roiling courage and he'll say yes. And I'll get handmade cards on Mother's Day that the dad will swear were the baby's idea. And six months before the baby turns nine, the dad will break up with me. And I'll be at the birthday party, the first time we'll have seen each other in months, and three days previous I'll have real-ized I'm pregnant. And I'll be filled with joy and terror at this party, standing with the other parents, excited to be one of them. In the first week of lockdown, he will paste a *You Are Not Alone* card onto my front window, and when 1 see it, very much alone, 1 will weep and wonder who did it, never imagining it could be him.

The Somatic Craze

TARA MICHELLE SUGGESTS THAT PERHAPS I'm over him but my nervous system isn't. Everyone talks about the nervous system lately, but I find the concept difficult to visualize. It's so satisfying to imagine your body doesn't have a role below the neck. A floating head, I say to my somatic therapist. She asks me to describe how my body feels right now. Like, do you want an adjective? It takes an hour for me to say, I don't know, I guess it feels uneven? If you feel your feelings physically in your body, you can release them. I spent the morning reading Lisa Robertson's *The Baudelaire Fractal* for the second time, but I do not understand how to answer this deceptively simple question. I'm not supposed to think of the answer, just notice the answer. Sometimes it feels as though I pay my therapist so that I can ask her, What does that even mean? over and over again. But when you email me after a year of not speaking, I feel it like an explosion in my chest and then realize, Oh, that's what she meant.

October

IT'S YOUR BIRTHDAY AND YOU'RE forty-four and we are estranged now. I'm up early because I'm about to let someone in the side door before the sun rises and this is the first birthday I haven't spent with you in six years, and before the soft knock I send you a happy birthday text in a gesture of goodwill though of course I shouldn't have. Even though there are others in my bed these days, I'm only here because you asked me to leave. I might cross that threshold, do a death drop in the middle of Bloor Street, staring up at the place we had breakfast a million times, with the plantains and the avocados, with hands touching across the table, with soccer flickering to my right, and the click of the streetcar behind me, and your full attention. The fullness of it.

Red Flags

THE FIRST TIME HE BROKE up with me, he gave me a handwritten, itemized list of things he didn't like about me. When I got upset, he gave me a list of things he loved and said he loved me again and why wasn't I answering the phone. It was on me that I didn't leave, but I was entranced. He seemed like everything I'd ever wanted in a person. You can't help timing, I'd told Andrea in the beginning, when I explained he was taking me away for a weekend. But you just started dating last week, she said. It's too soon. I was impermeable to logic.

He didn't like it when women published work about shame, desire, vulnerable things. He will hate this book, but he will never read it. I would be annoying during action films, constantly muttering, They're obviously not going to kill him. He's on the poster! The whole narrative wouldn't make sense! I was always saying the wrong things. My feelings were so big I was just stumbling through our life together, a messy chaos monster.

Twenty-Four Frames

I'M DRIVING HOME FROM A date, the kind of mediocre sex date I forced myself through in the name of moving on, and I'm listening to a country song that reminds me of you and how I can't let go. I remember leaving your new house that you hadn't yet moved into, riding my bike home because I didn't know how to drive then, replaying what had just happened over and over, the memory would stay in my muscles, in my breath. I would blush but it would feel involuntary. I would be washing a dish or picking up my mail, and the feeling of a hand around my wrists, or the whispers of things you would say, would appear as though a film flashback and I wouldn't be able to talk or take in the present moment.

Now I have good sex but I barely think about it later. I'll listen to a podcast and think, *Oh, they will find this interesting, I'll send them a link.* Or I'll see a dress she might like in a window and send her a photo. But I don't swoon. I don't feel taken or haunted or otherworldly. I don't find it lacking anymore, the further away I get from transcendence. I think that maybe this kind of connection is better, the kind that doesn't rearrange you, that doesn't careen so close to destruction. Maybe this is normal. Maybe it's not dull, maybe it's just not an addiction.

Valentine's Day 2020

THERE WERE ONLY FIVE MONTHS after the breakup and before the first lockdown. I was just starting to be myself again. I took a test. I was waiting to hear about a comedy-writing job that would take me to Los Angeles the following Monday, perhaps a chance to do Hollywood with a calmer heart. But something in me knew. I could barely fit my breasts into my job interview dress. If I was going to get on a plane, I needed to know for sure.

I set the timer and looked out at the sunrise over Christie Pits. In one reality I was pregnant, by a friend who didn't want a baby. I was still in love with someone who would never love me again. In that reality, I was entirely alone but I was also free. A million possibilities opened up. This felt euphoric.

In the other reality, I was not pregnant. I was lovers with someone who comforted me, I had a book nearly ready to go to print. My main task was to heal from the toxicity of my last relationship. I was alone but I was supposed to be alone. This life was also good, in its own way. In this life there was less magic, less fury, but there was joy. There was all of me.

When the little digital square said YES, like the screen of a 1980s robot wristwatch, I yelled so loudly my terminally ill cat jumped off the bed. I didn't get the job but I didn't care because I really liked being pregnant, like I had the strongest heart, like I could walk across the city kicking obstacles out of my way. I felt physically invincible, or like my body was doing something for the first time in my life.. Most of my work involves staying still. Thinking. Staring. Underlining passages and conjuring interiority of people who don't exist. But this cluster of cells was real. My body was building a baby, a person. I felt no pain. Only a surge toward the brave future.

Good Morning, Are We All Still Alive in Our Beds

ON MY FORTY-FOURTH BIRTHDAY I go for brunch with Andrea and Marcilyn in Liberty Village. We used to have a group text when we all lived alone that checked in every morning with *I didn't die in my sleep.* I tell them that I'm pregnant. They jump from their seats, faces in bloom, having witnessed my journey of indecision for over ten years. I have a photo of me blowing out a candle on a pancake. I remember telling them that I was a bit scared but mostly thrilled. I washed my hands in the bathroom extra-long because of the rumours that the coronavirus was here now and that we should be careful.

The last public gathering I go to before Covid hits is a Writers Guild panel discussion with Alison, the one I ate steaks with in Calgary at the lit festival in an earlier poem. It's been years since we last saw each other. We've both had some hits and misses with our careers and are trying to write for television because we like to have health insurance. She sits at the bar at the TIFF theatre and I decline a drink because I'm pregnant. There is often something that separates me from straight women writers who are mothers that I can't name, only feel, and when I'm pregnant this separation dissolves, because they know so much about being a parent and a writer at the same time. Even though I am still queer and planning to co-parent with my queer and trans friend, for those months I am transplanted into this world of babies and advice and direct messages from women who are also pregnant and want to tell me secret things.

55

We meet in person for the last time, so that I can tell you I'm pregnant in person, so that you don't hear it from someone else. I explain that Kaleb and I are going to co-parent, as friends. You post a photo on Instagram of a candle with a cryptic message about a pregnancy. I don't follow you but a mutual friend sends me a screencap. It's both touching and strange that you would share this. But I love your support.

Zero Percent Chance

I STARTED THIS WORLDWIDE EMERGENCY pregnant. According to the internet the chance of getting knocked up at forty-four was basically zero percent, but it happens on a strange autumn morning, in a way that feels like fate intervening in a romantic way. Not romantic in the usual sense, but the romance between myself and a baby, my own future life. Later that afternoon Paul drove me to a women's prison to give a talk about writing. I was scared to be locked inside so I slipped a chip of Ativan into my mouth in the parking lot. The women in the inmates' book club looked like teenagers or grandmothers, no in-between. He'd driven around Kitchener killing time while I tried to say anything meaningful about the book I didn't believe in anymore. I was nice to a serial killer, by accident. I'd said, *Good luck with your poetry*, and then I looked up her name when I got home and realized who she was. As he drove home, because I was still too scared of highway driving, I was buzzing from the feeling of being locked in somewhere. Back in the city, after I dropped him off, the first few piano plinks of "Runaway" by Kanye pinged off alleyway garages, dove through the high beams. I might have been too high to drive. Driving, like fucking a cis guy, was a new thing I mostly only did at sixteen and forty-four. But I felt something ethereal at that moment, like I'd shifted into a new lane in my life.

Lacrimal

PAUL DOESN'T WANT MUCH OF anything. I am always wanting: twelve tabs open above my manuscript, a set of gold-topped faux-vintage Gucci lipsticks, a getaway cottage with an outdoor hot tub, dresses that will disappoint when they don't arrive with the body. Paul makes yogourt out of sour milk; fixes all the broken things in my apartment so I don't have to deal with the landlord. When it gets cold he brings my bike inside and puts it on a stand, drills plant hooks in the ceiling. He leaves jokes for me in high places because I am four-foot-eleven and rarely look up because it makes me dizzy. A La Croix can on my highest shelf, his name scribbled in flour spilled on the oven fan from the baking cupboard above. These moments make me laugh; he would kill on social media, but he doesn't like being corny and open-hearted or asking for attention. I walk to the food co-op where he works just to see other humans and buy hippie chocolate bars and rose-scented laundry soap. So that when I get home I can write a scene or two of the feature film I'm faking my way through. Will this be a book of prayers? A liturgical cut line through this year of grey days.

How to Have Sex in a Pandemic

Paul duct-tapes clear recycling bags into a tent jacket and we hug, masked faces turned away, for fifteen seconds. This is as close to fucking as we've gotten in seventy-two days. The last time we had sex we were on his living room floor. I was three weeks pregnant and he said, You look so different, you smell so different, and it was animalistic and weird. He didn't want the baby but he was hungry. I always fall for masculine people who like grabbing at my breasts like drunk babies. They all get the same half-lidded looks. A look I'm jealous of because nothing gives me that look. Before the pandemic I went on a date with a femme to try to see if I might be able to feel that way. After all, it's a universal truth that the best part of watching porn is watching breasts go up and down. She gets up to order us beer, and I am too shy. I am mortified. I am too mortified to even know if I feel any attraction. Is this what straight men feel like? If I look at her with longing like that, will I scare her? I have never been scared of scaring someone I might want to kiss. I'm the one who gets kissed. Before you, I'd dated women for twenty years, but they were always on the masculine spectrum. That old joke about how lesbian bed death doesn't exist, it's just that too many bottoms are dating each other. Finding a top in a pandemic is even harder than finding a top in regular life.

When Paul leaves, the plastic-bag hug makes me energetic. I clean my kitchen, dancing around. That small human contact makes me high. The last time I let him in my house we'd watched a documentary and didn't touch and he complained about my cats and I was pregnant and he wished I wasn't. A week later when we were quarantined away and alone, we thought, That was so stupid. We should have fucked. Hindsight.

Every night at 6 p.m. one of the dads on my street skateboards shirtless back and forth in front of my house. It is a crime. When I go out and get on my bike in order to bike around in circles like a teenager to get some exercise, he says *Hi* real teenager-like. We both have bad tattoos from twenty years ago. We are strangers and both basically forty-five, I'm guessing. I haven't dated a cis straight man since I was twenty-one. Paul's body count for male lovers is higher than mine. There is a comfort in finally dating someone who is also bisexual. I never learn the skateboard guy's name.

I am so lonely, but the kind of slow-burn lonely where I walk from the bedroom to the kitchen to the living room, sending my group text *I Love You*s. I wonder how I got to be so alone. But being alone is so much more bearable. I bake treats and leave them on friends' porches. I read a romance novel for the first time because I need to skim along the surface of emotions, to get deeper would be ominous. I'm one of the lucky ones, working from home, ordering supplies, but I still feel as though we're all lying on the floor of the bank, waiting for the illness that's taken us hostage to decide what to do.

Spring 2021

A SPARROW ON THE SILL tears at the sign you taped to my window, pandemic week two. It read, *You Are Not Alone*, yet one year later I am more alone than I've ever been. Since I spent the first three months of my life in a machine that breathed for me. Now it's a one bedroom with two baby tigers, my two dead orchids, a frozen fertilized embryo from a girl in Kansas in a lab across town. The femme DMs me, *I'll be your experiment.*

These spare phrases are how I connect now, meditated desire, masked faces. Instead of finding a new partner, I decide to find a mortgage broker who won't turn me down. It takes a lot of pleading emails and phone calls before I find one who understands an artist's income. I spend my days looking at photos of houses I can't afford in small towns.

Disorganized
Attachment Blues

IN A BATH OF ROSE petals and geranium oil, I read a novel by a British writer I envy because she's not making the mistakes I made with my first books. I've been trying to figure out my problems with enjambment in poetry and my long history of not knowing when to cut things off. I will stay forever, I used to think. After you said something cruel, you confessed that you worried I would never leave you, even if I should. Now that you're gone, when someone new feels a thrill for me, my stomach turns. Do I only fall for people who keep their distance? Do I like the dance that drives me crazy? I dread the phone. I roll my eyes at what they like about me. How could they like these things about me? I remember the list he wrote of all my faults and the endless additions I've made to the list since then. Maybe I should embrace being a spinster. Do spinsters have flags? But the trouble is, I have so few hobbies. I like to read and write and watch films and see plays and have conversations and buy presents for people when they're not with me to surprise them, but the thing I like best is having a crush, being in love, asking people questions about what they believe and how their life has been so far and what they're afraid of and how brave they are with certain things and what do they value and do you like to read on a beach, do you want to read Zadie Smith's essay on the difference between joy and pleasure? I like people too much to be this afraid of people or afraid to love people. And the anxiety is not poetic. I download WhatsApp to speak to someone from Hinge and there is a string of texts between you and me that I'd forgotten about. It's all about whether or not one of your sons has lice and what I'm going to make for dinner. A reminder to pick up milk on your way home. I expect operatic exchanges, but I have to scroll far back to find anything that isn't about our weekly schedule, the house, a reminder to give the oldest cat his heart meds, the school play, the plans to visit your parents.

Topophobia

I CLOSE THE AIRPLANE WINDOW shades to block out the oblivion of sky. I like being squished on the inside of a restaurant booth. I like the middle seat of a canoe. I would be unfit psychologically for nearly every apocalypse scenario. I often say I'll be like the wife in Cormac McCarthy's *The Road* and just give up before anyone fights over a single can of expired beans. But in order to be a good citizen during the pandemic, I am asked to slide back into my worst habits: me, on the couch with my cats, a pile of books, endless television, finishing the internet. This is like an alcoholic being told to sip whisky all day for the sake of mankind. When I venture out to the pride parade, we slip our masks off in moments, and I shrink away from the breath stream of women screaming, No justice! No peace!

The End of Fear

AT SOME POINTS DURING THE pandemic she would get to the end of fear. She would stand in the driveway in her socked feet stuffed into sandals, oblivious to the winter wind, and ask her parents, Have you been inside with anyone? Should we test? She didn't feel like it though. She just wanted to share air with them and celebrate her birthday without the nasal swabs and fifteen-minute anxiety spiral, those things had consumed Christmas. She walks through Foodland with her mask on, but it's become normal now, to have it on her face, that chemical smell from its plastic casing. In 2021 she'd rushed through every grocery trip, diligently making a note in her phone of where she went and for how long and at what time. Now she sometimes lingers. She goes to the Dollarama and looks at plastic cups and clothes hangers she doesn't need. Just to be outside her home. But then hours later she thinks, *If I'm being too nonchalant, will the disease get me when I'm not paying attention?* She was mad before, and she is going madder every day, and sometimes she gets a reprieve from not caring, from not being able to care.

Heartbreak That Doesn't Fade with Time

I SIT IN MY CAR asking my phone for literary essays about grief that doesn't resolve. Heartbreak that doesn't fade with time. Sarah and Alex, who host a podcast, are talking to me the way they have been this entire pandemic. I get out of my car, which is filled with old coffee cups and lines of poetic surrender on the back of parking-lot receipts. I'm crying again but hardly register it. The further I get from people, the more secure I feel. The crying must be a message from my body that I'm not as safe without other humans as my mind imagines. I may be in control, but I am untethered. I could float away from my spot in front of the TV, where I think about intellectual bravery, whether I'd finally be proud of a novel if it was too smart to be sold in Costco. When you write books, you're always alone, but at least before I had the waitress at Universal Grill, where I'd read the *New Yorker* on Saturday mornings. She was the first stranger I told about my pregnancy because, Is the cheese raw or . . . ? I'm missing those incidental social interactions. Perhaps they sustained me. I am too comfortable being alone. When I'm not alone, I feel a nagging sense that I can never fully relax. I go on several dates in parks. I meet someone who, on paper, is everyone I'm looking for in a future partner—trans guy my age, funny, kind, likes kids—but every time we meet I get blinding headaches in one eye and a little tick tick tick in my head that reminds me, Wait, you do not want a partner. You cannot have one. You are not ready yet because you are still crazy with grief. You have to figure out why it's so hard for you to be a good partner. I drive home from the east end so grateful not to be witnessed. I want to wear these sweatpants forever, and if my house gets messy, I do not wish for commentary. I drop an olive on the floor. I pick it up the following Tuesday. I still have sex sometimes, but it is a solitary experience, our own minds orbiting the space. I have never been less in love. I have no intimacy with anyone, I tell Paul on the phone on a Sunday morning. He is the one I'm closest to, but the longer we are lovers, the more apart we are. I tell him that afternoon, I don't remember how to do this. I do, he says confidently. After sex we watch a Kelly Reichardt film and then walk on the ice outside by the sand dunes. He's so nimble ascending them as I watch from the beach, very still, slowly freezing.

Outlet Beach

I FIND OUT THE POET Minnie Bruce Pratt has passed away. It's the first time in a long time—years now—that I wish I could talk with you. I'm standing in wet sand. I used to tell you that I stood on the shore and you went in and out of our relationship like the tides. The waves right now are unbearably loud but the sun is a neural balm. My child would have been two today if she'd been more than a clump of cells. Who couldn't survive the seat warmers in my car, or the Ativan I took before I knew I was pregnant, or the asthma inhaler, or the stress of the first three weeks of the pandemic, or my being forty-three, something made her slip away. I just did one hour of therapy in the green chair I've been in since 2020 and I didn't talk about the due date, how it was today. And I didn't talk about your eldest son, who is sixteen today and was projected to share a birthday. I remember my hand against his forehead when he had a fever, on the top bunk. I remember it was hard for us to talk, he and I, and that I left the house on Beatrice Street disappointed in myself that we hadn't bonded the way I thought we would, like the step-parents and children do in movies, wishing I had been a better partner, better extra parent. I was around. I tried to be a warm presence but I think I just lingered, offering tofu dogs and sliced cucumbers and gift certificates for the local independent bookstore tucked into birthday cards. Today I text him *happy birthday* and he replies *thanks* with a heart emoji and I pull off the road to cry about how nice it was that he responded. Now I'm standing on the beach wishing I could have had a chance to know my baby. The poems I'd have read to her. Maybe she'd have learned to swim at this beach. The beach I've learned to be alone at.

Minnie Looking for My Leslie

WHAT DO YOU MISS, FRIENDS ask, years later. I miss his wit, his passions, the way he narrates the journey. I miss the crackle, the lucky feeling, of when we would reconnect. Now I leave after one date if there's instant banter or a sign of sparks sparks sparks. He sent *you are the best and no one else can have you.* And then two months later a list of all the things he doesn't like about me. Do you have regrets? asks a therapist. I wish I could go back to that moment, those ripped loose papers with black ink scrawled near illegible, and light them on fire. Then wake up the next day and look for someone who would never write a list like that. The trouble is I stayed and then turned into a person who might write a list like that.

Can I Tell You Some Facts about Rabies

I TELL PAUL I'VE WRITTEN pandemic poems about us, after warning him about how bats can bite you without you noticing and then you can die of rabies. There's a window of time where you can get a shot for it, but what if you don't know? I can't choose safety as an artist, even if it's my first choice in every other instance. Paul has been a donor for many queer couples. When I cat-sit for some friends, there are children's photos that kind of look a little like him all over the house, but it's weird to mention the biology of it all. We swing in the hammock by the tomato garden and talk about who we wish we could date if we weren't too crazy to date. I call him when my basement floods—What should I do? Get a bucket? I have my own house, a thing I never thought I'd have. And all I had to do was have everything in my life fall apart and write a few things I don't love. I should just surrender to the heartbreak of it all, I suppose, filling my sink with dirty water, mesmerized by the gritty swirls, the rotting air. I have a beautiful life without a baby, without a great enduring mythical type of love, but it's harder to narrativize. It's image-based: dirty hands, lists of Fun! Things! For! Winter!, stopping the car to watch rabbit families run, new day-by-day, no-illusions love.

Layover in the Winnipeg Airport

LEFT HAND GRIPS A MINI air purifier by its plastic handle, the right drags a coral suitcase of old reliable nightgowns, unread novels, dirty socks. The suitcase was hard to close around the bulge of a mug branded with the logo of the literary festival that paid for my flight. Chris watches me struggle to push it into the zipper's last gape.

I have two haptic memories of this airport. The grip of a descending escalator while talking to my agent, having decided which publisher to sign with while in the air. I watched the flight map on the small TV, feeling anxiolytic lightness while still aware, in moments, that this was a life-changing decision. I read my pros/cons list to you, as you looked up from your laptop, writing last minute a research paper with a poetic title. We were heading to an academic conference. I only ever really enjoyed hearing your papers. I judged scholars harshly—those repetitive adjectives, the self-effacing preambles—everyone else's writing was weak and unengaging, except yours. I no longer recommend falling in love with another writer.

The other memory is of blurred vision, heavy chest, both lifting at the sight of you in the arrivals area. I'd heard about Alex's death just before takeoff. I was in Winnipeg to give a talk. We walked from the Forks to the Osborne Bridge and I bought a mug shaped like an owl that Alex would've liked and your friend was having delusions and you bought them winter boots and the whole grey city felt like it was mourning with us. In moments it felt as though not having delusions was less sane. The big questions at the heart of your intellectual work were often about how to shift power, how to look at ableist assumptions we make about what we value. I remember how tenderly you cared for your friend and thought there is no one with a more expansive heart. And then, of course, months later wonder why there isn't that same tenderness for me. Scarcity inflates value, I guess.

I'm riding shotgun in a rental pickup truck when we pass a street where Chris tells me he was once mugged at knifepoint. He is very casual about this story. I am trying to be a person who can be more casual about a lot of things and, at the same time, someone who can feel their emotions instead of denying them, let them settle in my body. Outside the city a field of dead sunflowers looks like an army of aliens. That night I meet a donkey called Celine Dionkey. What I'm trying to say, I suppose, is that life goes on.

Acknowledgements

Thank you to Joe, Ange, Will, Lisa, Paul, Marcilyn, and Andrea.

Thank you to Natalie for the beautiful cover and for being my first Prince Edward County friend.

Thank you to Amber Dawn, Ali Blythe, and Hannah Green for your beautiful endorsements.

Thank you to the poet Ariana Reines, who I don't know, for writing the collection *Coeur de Lion*, which inspired this book.

Thank you to Hazel and Jay Millar at Book*hug for taking a chance on this manuscript when it was a pile of twigs and dirt, and to Jacob McArthur Mooney, whose keen editorial acumen made it into an actual book. Thank you to Brittany Landry and Reid Millar and everyone else at Book*hug for your work.

About the Author

PHOTO CREDIT: N MAXWELL LANDER

ZOE WHITTALL is the author of the short story collection *Wild Failure*, and five bestselling novels: *The Fake, The Spectacular, The Best Kind of People, Holding Still for as Long as Possible,* and *Bottle Rocket Hearts.* Her previous poetry collections include *Pre-cordial Thump, The Emily Valentine Poems,* and *The Best Ten Minutes of Your Life.* Her work has won a Lambda Literary Award and the Writers' Trust Dayne Ogilvie Award, and been shortlisted for the Scotiabank Giller Prize. She has worked as a TV writer on the Emmy Award–winning comedy show *Schitt's Creek* and *The Baroness von Sketch Show,* for which she won a 2018 Canadian Screen Award. She was born in the Eastern Townships of Quebec and now lives in Prince Edward County, Ontario.

Colophon

Manufactured as the first edition of
No Credit River
in the fall of 2024 by Book*hug Press

Edited for the press by Jacob McArthur Mooney
Copy-edited by Jo Ramsay
Proofread by Stuart Ross
Type + design by Michel Vrana
Cover image: *Crying Girl No 1 (with Intentional Bitch Face)* by
Ambivalently Yours; used with permission
Printed in Canada
bookhugpress.ca